KU-618-730

Finding the
Relationship you Deserve

Rosie O'Hara

I dedicate this book, and my heartfelt thanks go to my partner Jim Symon, who is very long suffering and not quite believing I was writing a book and not working on the laptop (nor that his name is mentioned in it, just a few times), to my friend and confidante Linda Birnie without whom many things would not have happened (and thanks to the people who were instrumental in training her), to my daughter and best mate Kristin Rietsch, my lovely grandsons Leon and Nico, to my son Jacob O'Hara (who once told me "all men are not useless — you just haven't met a useful one, yet" — and he was right!), to the late and much missed by all of us, Michael O'Hara (and his children Tracy and Darren), to Karen Douglas and Joanna Pirie (who both also encouraged me to write this book), to my hairdresser Claire Gardner (every woman needs a good hairdresser), and to my first husband Klaus Rietsch (thanks for the lessons learned).

My thanks also to John Seymour who wrote to me "May your life be filled with delightful surprises," and it is, and to Claire Rayner whose advice I remember and share with you in this book.

And my acknowledgements to:

Those people of the NLP world, Richard Bandler and John Grinder, John Seymour (who pointed out to me I'd never had time to have a mid-life crisis, as life kept on getting in the way), Cricket Kemp and all at NLP Northeast who set me on the road to NLP, L. Michael Hall, Shelle Rose-Charvet, Joseph O'Connor, Robin Prior, Wyatt Woodsmall and all those people in the NLP world, too numerous to mention who I have come across and learned from.

My thanks go to Sir Tim Rice for giving me his permission to quote from "I know him so well" (on page 92) from the musical Chess, the copyright for this song is owned by 64 Squares Music.

Contents

Why did I write this book?

I spent a large part of my life in some interesting relation-ships, not necessarily useful for me and perhaps not for the other person, but interesting. Do you know why? Because I spent a large part of my life concentrating on what I didn't want - and that's exactly what I got! Several times.

And whilst writing some emails to my friend Jaclyn who now lives abroad, and telling her about what I have discovered in my life, she asked? "Why don't you write a book about how you got this great relationship you have now? After all you've got something worth more than any money can buy and you can share with other people how to do it too!

So, here it is, a transcript of the emails I sent and she asked some questions, but I wrote it as a book. It also gives you some tried and tested tips on how to get what you want, what you really, really want, perhaps I'll tell you about some of things I did that didn't work out and how — with hindsight, I could have done things differently.

Finding the
Relationship you Deserve

Let's perhaps first cover some things that you might think get in the way, or that might be getting in your way and you might think they're not really getting in the way. Well just a bit, maybe?

You've not got the best figure? (This covers by the way too short, too tall, too fat etc.)

You're too old?

You haven't got ....?

You have children.

You have grandchildren.

You have a ....(insert pet)

You have a .... or are ....

We could go on................

However, beware;

If you have bad breath, a liking for drink, spicy foods, fetishes, horror movies and other things that other people might find a problem - you just might either need to find someone who likes exactly the same things or take other action first.

Important is - you are happy with yourself, so you have good self esteem, well most of the time, we might aspire to be perfect — perfect figure, perfect at cooking, making love, playing football, or whatever or we might not, but it's really useful if most of the time we can be happy with ourselves.

So my story is, latterly widowed mum of 2 grown up children, granny to 2 beautiful boys (hey they're my grandsons), like reading, like films, like jazz, like to cook and reckon I can do it pretty well, like to swim, like to make things (when I find the time), I speak a second language fluently, ride a motorbike occasionally, I know lots about losing weight, I know lots of things (not often useful to most people) and most important I think, is that I like people and what makes them tick. Downsides, opinionated, I will say what I think (doh), and sometimes I'm starting to sound like my mother. According to some people I can't sing, according to others I can, according to some people I might be all sorts of things. But that's life.

Now I know I'm good at my job, in part because I get personal satisfaction from what I do, and I see other people benefiting from what I do and I hear what they say, and I get really good feelings when I read some of things people write about me and my work (not always — I'm human you know). I also know I'm good at my job because other people tell me, sometimes it's the clients I work with, sometimes it's my peers and assistants, sometimes someone tells me they've heard something good about me, and how what I did with them worked for them and sometimes it took them a while for that to work for them.

In that last paragraph I wrote about the fact that sometimes I know myself that something has been good —
Do you know yourself that something went well, or do you

need someone or other people to tell you that something went well or show you in some way?

There's no right or wrong but it is useful to know and check. If you're always telling yourself you're good at something, you might be wrong sometimes and also other people might regard you as being "full of yourself", or "not interested in other people" or something else, so might it be useful to notice other people and ask their opinion. You know, ask a mate, phone a friend, or ask the audience. And hell that's really useful if you want a relationship, to notice what other people's opinions of you are, as we might need to see things from our new or prospective partner's point of view, or hear what they are saying, and notice that they have feelings too!

So what next? Or perhaps what first?

Well be clear, be very, very clear about what you want, as I mentioned earlier knowing what we don't want is all very well, but if you focus on just that, what you don't want, that's what you'll get. That's ok if you want to confirm your Belief "that nothing good ever happens to me" or "I always meet the wrong man/woman" and notice, if, like me, you are into music and most of us are in some way and many of us have an "Our tune" or "I remember exactly where I was when I first heard that tune (and who I was with possibly)", then some lyrics are not really useful "On my own, how can I exist without you?", "What do I do to make you love me?", "As long as he needs me." – mm we can do really effective, but not really useful "programming" of our brains with that stuff – notice it and enjoy it as a song, but not as a creed by which I live.

Our beliefs have a major impact on our lives.

The Things We Believe

Beliefs are thoughts that form our reality. They are thoughts we consider to be true, created through our senses, our filters (the way in which experience, see or hear or feel things), our emotions, and by deleting, distorting and generalising. Beliefs are filters, we filter our experiences through our beliefs, and we generally only (but not always) pay attention to experiences that support our beliefs. As our beliefs act as our filters, our thoughts (internal representations) are affected by them and so they influence our physiology (that's the way we stand or sit, aches and pains can also be affected by our beliefs), state (you know this thing "I'm in a state", well you can have a useful one (a state) you know, I'll tell you how later).

Belief

I am no good at meeting people

Thoughts

Oh no, it's going to be like every other time, I'll mess it up.

State

Nervous, anxious, butterflies in stomach, or some such.

Behaviour

If you are nervous when meeting people you are likely to avoid eye contact, speak quickly or not all, breathe rapidly and display lack of engagement with the person you are attempting to speak to. Or stand like "a wallflower" in the corner.

Consequences

People you meet will not find you engaging or you will not meet anyone.

The result is that your belief that you are no good at meeting people is reinforced. What happens is we behave in a way that meets up with our beliefs, and prove to ourselves we were right to have that belief in the first place.

If for example you believe that people will react unfavourably towards you, then you will give off unconscious signals to this effect and the response you will get will reaffirm this.

If you believe you are bad at sports, cooking, driving, writing letters (I met someone who thought because he "couldn't write a letter the right way first time, he was useless at writing letters" (it's always useful to check your letters for errors, typos, wrong information and perhaps leave it overnight)), you will look for examples to confirm this and dismiss any examples that prove the contrary.

Some people's beliefs are so strong and become such a habit that other people get carried along with this. I once had a lodger who believed other people always acted unfairly towards her, and shouted at her and then I ended up in a situation where I started to behave like this and shouted at her!

All over a plastic bag.

Our brains recode every single event of our lives; this has been well documented since the 1950s. This includes verbal messages we hear around us even when we are not actively paying attention and they go straight to the unconscious mind. The same applies to those things we constantly repeat to ourselves – "You stupid fool", "I know I'll mess it up."

Messages are given to us (and we give them to others - our children, our work colleagues, our partners) as a form of hypnosis, and if we or they hear them often enough they become true.

Eeek!

So when I was on my own and believed that guys weren't interested in me, because I was independent (and I still am) and could look after myself perfectly well, I didn't need a man, certainly not one who wanted to sponge off me and laze around all day watching TV, smoking cigarettes, was work-shy, no good at odd jobs, didn't have his own car, didn't like my friends, was jealous of the fact that I have friends (in some very odd places) – a man once asked me if I had any normal friends? I had to check out his criteria for normal – it was they liked a drink, well lots of drinks, they liked to get off their faces on drink and smoke a lot and be generally miserable and have "real jobs" (I have a friend who is a crane driver, but many of them are musicians (one of them is a carpenter as well), trainers, lawyers, a professor, store detective (not sure what was "real" according to that particular man).

Well guess what I got in my life? Ah yes and there's another one, I didn't want a man who was married, or in any kind of relationship (I value exclusivity). I got exactly what I was concentrating on, most of the time (well not always exactly, but fulfilling most of the above things I was thinking I didn't want), because they were the things I actually concentrated on.

So with a little help from some friends I set up a list of criteria that I wanted and here they are:

1. Single, with no needy appendages (that means no wife, fiancé, no relatives he might need to dash off to when we've arranged to do something)
2. Own house
3. Own car (these are not in order of ranking by the way)
4. Own money, so needs to have a job or some form of independent income
5. Wears shoes (not smelly trainers in case you are wondering, and not tatty shoes)
6. Knows about personal hygiene and how to have a shower and use soap etc. at least once a day (specifics are important)
7. Knows that different clothes are appropriate for different occasions
8. Likes music, not necessarily my music
9. Appreciates I have a job and that I work odd hours and he's okay with that
10. Likes to travel
11. Is fun to be with and has a sense of humour
12. Likes children and perhaps has some grandchildren around too
13. Likes people and gets on with them
14. Likes animals but does not particularly own a dog
15. Has his own interests and appreciates that I have mine
16. Wants to do things together with me, try new things out

17. Likes closeness and hugs
18. Is open
19. Is truthful
20. Can stand up to me, I can be bossy and I get on my soapbox
21. Non-smoker
22. Likes to eat good food
23. Doesn't get drunk on a regular basis
24. Wearing a kilt would be a bonus
25. Ah yes and likes sex (with me – only)

Now you can have a list saying whatever you wish for, I have a friend for whom it was very important that the guy (she has now married) had a full head of hair, I thought she was being a bit picky, but now I don't think so, she just knew what she wanted. And for her, her list included he had to like dogs and a few other things.

> So list at least 20 things that would be important to you in a partner, you might be vegetarian, you might have certain religious or political views, and you might want to make sure your partner has the same ones (saves wars at home), you might want children, to travel the world, you hate cheese – anything you want in a partner list it - remember people don't change. They might tell you something you want to hear, "yes I'd love to go to Germany with you" was one I often used to hear, but in reality they'd rather go to Majorca, "yes I'll look after the house whilst you are out at work" (and sell your CDs whilst you're out, or invite a few friends round for a boozy afternoon).

So your list says	
1	
2	
3	
4	
5	
6	
7	
8	
9	
10	
11	
12	
13	
14	
15	
16	
17	
18	
19	
20	

You can add more, you can take them away, and you can build your list up over a few days or a few months. I'll leave that with you for the moment.

When you've listed these things, take a look at them one by one and ask yourself so what would it be like if I met someone who didn't have their own house (they might not have to own it), but check also are they on the verge of declaring themselves bankrupt, have they actually got any money, are they looking for someone else to move in with?

A good friend of mine once met a man, who told her he owed a great deal of money, and had defaulted on his mortgage, and many other things. And he also told her, he would be happy to move in with her and run the house whilst she worked. Well he did move in, but he also expected her to earn the money, and that he could sit outside in his shed, and play darts and smoke, and she could work and paid all the bills. She hadn't really paid attention to what she really wanted (they also had absolutely nothing in common) — but reality was she wanted to feel wanted (not in the way he wanted her) and he wanted a roof over his head and a way of surviving without having to be accountable for it. Sad but true. She did get out of the relationship and started to pay better attention.

So check does this future partner really like to travel say, have they been abroad or wherever it is you like to go? Or are they just saying they might like to and don't really know and if they do go abroad, do they want adventure or do they want to have their fish and chips or very British tea abroad? What do you want when you go abroad?

It's quite a good idea not to live in one another's pockets, and not to have that expectation that the other person wants you there all the time, or that you need to be with them all the time. So some of the things on your list, how important are they in respect of your future partner? Do you want someone who shares the same interests as you? For me I wasn't particularly interested in someone having the same professional interests as me, as I didn't want competitiveness or one-upmanship, I'm not interested in these games of "mine's bigger than yours" . Also I'm used to the fact that not everyone speaks or reads fluent German and I don't necessarily need that as a permanent part of my life, it has been in the past and it's not that important to me as an everyday feature, I can read in German, watch DVDs and go to Germany with my partner to visit friends and relatives over there.

Check out what you want in a partner so for example - if you want a non-smoker and you have smoked in the past, compromising to be with smoker could mean a) you might start smoking again or b) you could be one of these dogmatic reformed smokers who makes their partner's life hell. Neither of which is very good, I think you'll agree. And if you've never smoked, the smoking could be an equal problem. Because no matter how much someone says they will give up something for you — it's a) very difficult for them and b) very stressful for both of you if you then start to use phrases like "you promised me", or "the fact that you don't give up means you can't possibly love me" — those are good ways to break a relationship. And please note even if you are good at "willpower" not everyone is, in fact most of us aren't and our reasons for the patterns or habits we run, or have are very deep seated and enforced changing of them for someone else is really hard.

On the other hand shared interests are very important for some relationships and are part of the "glue" that keeps things together and sometimes a good basis to start, but more on that in the next section.

Meeting People

Remember I mentioned the phrase "I can't meet people", "I can't possibly go there I won't know anybody" as someone once said to me. There are two possibilities in that last statement, if you don't go you will never know if there was someone there you knew and you will also never know if the most interesting person in you life might have been there. Have you tried thinking to yourself, I'm going there to get something out of the event – now what you want to get out of the event will depend on if the event is a social one or a business one. So think about what you want to get out of the event. What might that be, and can you be happy with something else? Now what's the something going to be? You could set yourself a goal of "I'm going there to meet a future life partner, mate, someone to have fun with, a business contact". If you are over specific, one of the downfalls could be that you decide on one of those things and you might still unconsciously be looking out for all of those attributes in the past that you don't want, so you come away and you think, aw that was rubbish, I didn't meet anyone. The fact is you probably did meet several people, (unless you refused to speak to anyone) but your filters were set to find either things you think are wrong or bad, or you just looked for people you already know and either spoke to them or avoided them like the plague.

So two ways of dealing with this or making things better. You could go there in the frame of mind "I don't know what I'm going to get out of this event, and I am sure that something good will come of it." After all sometimes if people don't actually know you are interested in finding a relationship, they might not let you know that they have a friend who too is looking for a relationship, or if this is a business event, having a good conversation with someone and telling them what you do and helping them to understand you are a nice person, will mean that when one of their mates or business colleagues mentions they are looking for someone who can.......... they will think of you. People like recommendations that's why there are dating agencies and that's why there are employment agencies. But bear in mind people can sometimes embellish the truth to dating agencies and employment agencies. Therefore generally when someone recommends a friend or someone from their close circle they will probably know more about that person, unless they are totally unscrupulous or also not filtering, but they are more likely to know if their mate is married or in a relationship, dating agencies don't actually check that. (The same applies to online dating too – I've often wondered how many people check what it is their partner is doing in front of the computer screen and exactly which joystick they have in their hands). So going to the event or club meeting to get to know people is a good way of letting people know that you are single or finding out if others are single.

Now if you are nervous or whatever way you want to describe it, and getting yourself into a state, there are ways of creating a good and resourceful state. Take a look at the next section and use the technique, work on it and it will give you a little piece of magic to help you be calm and cool and notice what is going on around you. It works.

Remember it requires practice. Only perfect practice makes perfect!

A Good and Resourceful State

Now remember I mentioned being in a good, and useful, and resourceful state?

Well would you like to have one of those that you can call up any time, any place, anywhere?

Here's how

1) Stand up and think back to a time when you were very confident, when you achieved something really good. Relive that moment, seeing what you see, hearing what you hear and feeling what you feel.

Briefly think about something else,
like what did you have for breakfast (or should you
have had)?

2) Relive that moment, see what you see (or what you are seeing), with any colours, any pictures, any scenery, any people and anything that was around, only you can know what this was. Hear what you hear (or what you are hearing),

any sounds that are particularly important to you at this time, anything you said to yourself or someone else said to you, as is appropriate for this "wow" experience. And then finally feel what you feel at that time, where are the feelings, in your body, all around you?

Briefly think about something else,

like what did you have for lunch (or should you have had)?

3) Go back and experience all of that again and then turn it all up, the sights, the sounds, the feelings, as if you have a remote control, or a dial, or a slide bar on a computer screen – turn it all up as far as is still comfortable.

Briefly think about something else, like your phone number backwards

4) As you feel the confidence building up inside you, imagine a circle on the floor just in front of you and colour this in with whatever colour you like.

Does it need to have a sound as well that indicates how powerful it is (only you can hear the sound)? Step into that circle taking all the sights, sounds and feelings with you.

When that feeling of confidence is at its fullest, step out of that circle, leaving those confident feelings inside the circle.

Briefly think about something else,
like what did you have for breakfast (or should you have had)?

5) Now think of a time in your future when you want to have that same feeling of confidence. See and hear what will be there just before you want to feel confident. This could be the door of a meeting room, answering the phone etc.

6) As soon as these cues are clear in your mind, step back into the circle and feel those confident feelings. Imagine that situation unfolding around you in the future with these confident feelings fully available to you.

Now step out of the circle again, leaving the confident feelings in the circle. Whilst outside -take a moment to think of that event in the future. Those confident feelings will come to you automatically. You've already reprogrammed yourself for that future event. You're feeling better about it and it hasn't even happened. When it does you will naturally respond more confidently.

If you find that difficult – some tips

If the difficulty is in finding a really wow moment, can you think of someone you know and admire who is really confident? They could be a real person, or TV, or film character (if you have any children you might use this circle for confidence and use Harry Potter, Tracy Beaker or whoever else is their idol) and create what that character will be seeing, hearing and feeling in the same way.

If stepping into the circle is an issue, then once you've got that supreme state see a colour in front of you and touch the seam on your trousers or skirt just as you get to the peak time and know that you can do that any time you want to get this state of confidence back again. Or other things you can do are imagine you are stepping through a doorway, or arch, switching spotlights on.

It works, you have to practise though and you can do this in the privacy of your own home, and practise often, only "perfect practice makes perfect" you know.

I've done this now for years and I have a "one size fits all" circle that I use for many occasions, usually when meeting people in business situations or presenting and sometimes when meeting people in social situations especially if I would rather be somewhere else. But you can have a circle for each different occasion if you want, you can chain circles together (might be useful to get you to the door of this place you want to meet Mr or Miss Right). No one else needs to know.

If the visualising, the seeing bit seems to be a little difficult then see yourself on a screen, put yourself in your favourite film (it might need a little practice, but it's worth it).

Okay so now you know how to create a good and useful state, you have confidence to get you to somewhere, and you can be cool, calm and collected. If you need some tips on how to be cool, calm and collected - just imagine you can be cool, calm and collected and practise this, think cool thoughts, a drink with ice in it, mountain stream, an open window with a cool breeze, whatever means cool to you will work, keep on seeing it, hearing it and feeling, either all three or whatever works best for you, it can take as many as 30 to 90 times to "reprogram" your thinking and behaviour in this way and when it is reprogramed just think of the rewards you will get.

Imagine now what it will be like when you meet this person you are going to have a relationship with, you may be fairly clear about what they will look like, how tall/short they will be, what colour hair, eyes, what kind of build.

You may not be clear — I don't have a "type" — my first husband (biography at the end of this book if you want to rush back there and find out why she has had all these men and can she really keep them!) — was 5ft 4ins and dark blonde hair, blue eyes, medium build, my second husband 5ft 8ins, jet black hair, wore glasses, brown eyes, slim build. My partner Jim is 6ft, balding grey/black hair (I forgot to put hair on my wish list), blue eyes, broad shoulders slim waist (well maybe not since he met me), slim legs and a paunch (age, good food and drink), wears the kilt.

Or, like me, what this partner looks like may not be an issue as the other things may be more important, but be clear, very, very clear. What will you see when you meet this person or when they are around? What will you hear? What will you feel?

For me I knew I would see bright colours, lots of people, I would hear laughter and music, the sound of voices and feel warmth.

If you want to, you could create a Vision Board, take pictures out of magazines, or photos you have, and cut out the pieces you want and create a vision, or a collage of what life will be like with this person, notice the colours, will there be music, do you want to add pieces of fabric or flowers, how do you want to embellish it? Avoid concentrating on one particular person – just because you cut out pictures of your favourite pop star, film idol, sportsperson - does not mean you will get to be with that person and worst case scenario you might be accused of having a fetish or stalking someone!

Keep this Vision Board somewhere where you can look at it on a daily basis, add to it, make a new one, if you do keep the old one, put it away and look at it some years later, to check what has actually happened in your life.

Before you go off to search around, or go to a meeting, or a prospective meeting do you need to do some work on stuff in the past that gets in the way sometimes?

Let's think about time.

Time

Time does not exist as a thing, yet we constantly talk about time as if it were a real thing that exists. Time is a way of labelling dark as night and light as day, having days and months etc. which we name. We cannot experience time directly by seeing, hearing or feeling it. We notice that things have changed - the daylight, darkness, changes in the weather, aging - growing children, shrinking seniors.

Time is a process in which we exist; we have to have ways of marking it out, such as days and months. We can get stuck in time and this helps us to create stuck states. We are all Time Travellers, we trip backwards and forwards in time, in our minds. Going back to our past in our minds and letting events there hold us back is not always useful. Yes, certain things will prevent us from making the same mistake, but what would it be like to learn from your mistake(s) - and to move on (as we say) in time and come into the present?— there's no such thing as failure, there's only feedback.[1] Bearing in mind of course that the present has just ceased to exist, because I've typed some more words or because you have just read some more of the words I have typed.

---

[1] 'There's no such thing as failure, there's only feedback" is one of the NLP Presuppositions or Operating Beliefs

We can also live too much in the future, taking a journey forwards to worry, or preoccupy ourselves with what might happen.

NLP[2] has skills and techniques with which we can find out how we code the past and future, those scenes we visit on our time travel and those events we worry about either because they have happened or they might happen. We can use these techniques to help us discover how we code the images we store of the past, or what it is we say to ourselves, that keeps us so effectively stuck. We can also discover how we can change the feelings that we use so effectively to tell us how to think about how we are going to behave. By that I mean the way we plan things - either by seeing images, or talking to ourselves, or playing tape loops of our voice, or creating the wrong feelings, because we "know" how to do it that way based on past experience, as we busily travel about in the past.

Time Travelling
and Unravelling

We are all Time Travellers, the fact that at any given moment in time we are alive and experiencing some kind of alive experience proves that. "?*?*?*?" you might be asking. Well, as, or whilst we sleep the earth moves and the clock moves, and that label we use of "time" shows or says to us, it's now 30 seconds later than it was, or 10 minutes, 2 hours, or a day etc. We use the labels we have for time to help us have a "path by which to steer", a way of orientating ourselves through life. And how often do we get stuck in the wrong time zone? How many of us allow the past to hold us back, hold us down?

By using language such as:

I do this because as a child, such and such happened
I do this because as a child, someone said .... to me
Someone I meet reminds me of someone else in my past, they speak in a certain tone, they look at us in a certain way - therefore I have to react in a certain way.
You have to understand all of things that happened to me make me react in this way.

Would it be more useful to be in the here and now?

Being in the Present

"Only the present moment exists."

Yesterday doesn't exist, except as a memory. You know memories are very unreliable. When you experienced yesterday, it was n-o-w. Tomorrow doesn't exist either, except in your imagination. When you experience tomorrow, it will be n-o-w. And as it's all that exists, it's a good idea to experience it, so...

How to do this - Sit with your feet flat on the floor, in a comfortable, centred position (spine straight, hands on your thighs or at your sides, breathing comfortably.) With your eyes open or closed, allow yourself to become aware of the different sounds, sights, smells & sensations around you. This is the present moment. Your present.

There are a number of good reasons for keeping your awareness in the present as much as possible.

There's a whole lot more on offer for you.

If you stop for a moment, you will realise that all the experiences of your life will always take place in a present moment. The more comfortable you are with the present moment, the more comfortable you'll be with those future presents.

The present is where you are.

If in doubt, look down at your body from where you are. Your body only exists in the present moment. Because it's there - so...

The present is the only time you can take action.

You can wish you did something yesterday, but yesterday no longer exists, so it will remain a wish. You can plan to take action in the future, but when you take the action, it will be in the present moment. The only time you can take action is in this second.

Wherever or whoever you're headed for, you presumably want to enjoy it when you get there. Get in the habit of enjoying the present now and you'll be even better at enjoying then when you get there.

Next - Gently place the tip of your tongue against the roof of your mouth just behind your front teeth (continue to breathe easily). Imagine you are holding a tiny bubble of oil (you can flavour it if you like) between the tip of your tongue & the roof of your mouth.

Doing this means you can't "talk to yourself" — the never ending voice that goes on in your head — I bet you can all think of one. ☺

Bringing your attention & energy into the present moment, means you can accomplish things more quickly, solve problems more effectively, & enjoy the process more than you might expect.

Tip - Before starting an important task, take a moment to centre yourself & relax. Then, get clear about what you want to accomplish, and then begin.

Baggage

You've heard the expression someone has baggage or issues. So, we all do at some point. What are you going to do about yours?

Now some people think it's a point for debate whether you take baggage with you on a journey and for those of you who travel by air (and if you haven't yet that's fine we can just imagine --) take a moment to think about the fact that you put your baggage on a belt and it goes into the hold of the plane and how about if it never came out again?

Tip

Imagine a line on the floor in front of you, the past is at one end, and the future at the other, somewhere along that line is the present. Looking at that line from where you are now, notice all that baggage, stuff from the past, that's the stuff you allow to get in the way when you think about relationships, the stuff that you let hang onto your ankles and pull you back! After all it's much easier to think about those things that have been going wrong, or have gone wrong repeatedly in the past in your relationships, after all you know that kind of stuff, don't you? This new stuff — it's hard, and what if.............................?

Well let's go for it, it will work and you just have to practise and you might think it's alright for her, but I had to
practise too.

So all that stuff in the past, how can you put it in the past,
how can you make sure that it stays there?

The line on the floor, check that all the baggage is in the
past, you can do this by either really stepping on this im-
aginary line on the floor, or by doing so in your head.
Once you've "stepped" on this line then check out that all
the baggage, the un-useful things you used to spend time
on, that used to come and trip you up, catch you out, is in
the past. So when you turn and face towards the future
none of that stuff is out there either in your present or in
your future.

Step off the line and look at this line in the past with the
"baggage'" on, check you really want to say farewell to
it, and now notice that in your mind's eye you can dispatch
all of this "baggage" along a conveyor belt, and notice
how it disappears off into the distance, and how it becomes fuzzy and unrecognisable and any colours that it
had, fade away, and hear yourself saying goodbye (or
any other phrases you may choose) and notice how you
can so easily let go of all the feelings that were attached
to that baggage and how you become lighter and happier
and that all of that baggage has disappeared into a huge
hold somewhere in another universe and is gone for ever.

(If for some reason you let it sneak back, please notice it's only you letting this happen and you actually have control and the right to send it back again — we sometimes need extra practice to unprogram all this bad stuff that we do extremely well.) A bit like defragmenting the computer, or rewriting a disk, or erasing something and starting all over again).

And remember that you now have plenty of space in your life, your mind, your world, your head, for exciting new things to come in, maybe some of the ones from the Vision Board you created earlier?!

Where can I meet someone?

Some people are lucky and after lots of searching they find the right person through a dating agency, online, at speed dating, at a singles club. Others don't.

One of the best pieces of advice I ever heard was from Claire Rayner at the time she was on Wogan's TV show and it was around Valentine's Day and I guess it was 1991. She was interviewed along with some other people and her suggestion for finding love was: "Join a club where people do something you like." Her reasoning was "even if you don't find love, you'll meet other people with whom you have a common interest, enjoy the shared interest and make friends". Well I tried that out and I can tell you she was right (and I also found love – you can go to the end of this book if you like to find out more about this or read on here).

You know you might sit at home and say I never meet anybody new, interesting or whoever you think you never meet. Mmm does the fact that you are sitting at home give you a clue as to why you aren't meeting anyone, yet? There are plenty of places and events around for you to meet people.

What stops you from going?

Is it easier for you to work and use work as an excuse?

What would you like to learn that you can't do yet?

What did you enjoy when you were younger?

What skill have you got you can share with others? Join a volunteer group. (Remember if it's full of older people don't write it off. Some of the oldies but goodies have families; there might be a single person in their family. Remember if you are older, that's all you are, older, but not dead yet and you have a right to a relationship too).

Let people know what you are looking for, ok not with a sign on your forehead, or by lusting over single (or not) people of the type you are you're looking for, but slip in your conversation that you are single, "yes I can be there, I can do that, I'm single at the moment [in this "pass the salt please" tone]" that way you're letting people know you can be there and are happy to be there, and also by the way I'm single at the moment. It allows them know you are perhaps you are open to a relationship. And beware — saying "I'm not interested" can also lead some people to believe they need to help you! (the brain has problems processing a negative at times). The same pass the salt tone will do if you receive any unwelcome advances, such as from a person of a sex you are not interested in, whether that be same sex or opposite sex, simply say "oh thanks, I'm really flattered but you're not my type".

So now you've stopped sitting at home and you're out and about and guys, please note if you want to meet girls it might be an idea to do something different to standard guy things (girls too, but girls are more likely to know people who are free and looking and to talk about that fact, guys not necessarily). There is a shortage of guys at most things, so there must be a surplus of women, and at least you get to learn something new, and something new about women if you listen to what they have to say to one another and to you, and you might not meet someone there, but someone there might have a friend. It's all about knowing a man or a woman who knows a man or a woman who...........

So like Claire Rayner said, you'll meet new friends and learn something new.

And if you always do what you've always done, you'll get what you've always got.

So having sorted out the baggage and got a good and resourceful state, where will you go? And more importantly when will you go?

Starting a Conversation

Okay so you're out there and you need to chat, "Dutch courage" (having a drink beforehand) is not really good for many reasons; I think you can work them out for yourself.

So what do I say?

> Well "hi" or "hello", "my name's ....", and when they tell you their name, repeat that name in your head and if you like, mentally write the name on that person's face (in your mind of course).

There's nothing worse than having a long chat with someone, and oops I can't remember what your name is. You've seen the ads "desperately seeking pretty girl I met at a bus stop in South Cheam or wherever", remember the name.

Ask them things like,

> "Have you been before?", "Do you like it here?", "How did you get here today/tonight?" and then ask them about what they do or what they are really interested in in life, and say that's interesting, tell me more. This way you will learn something about that person, you'll know what it's like when their face "lights up", what they are like when

they are happy, some people are happy at work, others not. You'll also learn do we have something in common and you'll also possibly learn something new. If they tell you about an achievement, say "well done", "wow I'm impressed" and look as if you are and sound as if you are too.

This way you'll start as you mean to go on, being interested and listening. If they don't ask about you about yourself, there are a few things to take into consideration:

♥ they may be too nervous to ask,

♥ and they may forget because of they are nervous,

♥ they may never have come across anyone who is interested enough to ask them about themselves and forget to ask about you,

♥ they may not be interested in other people at all (and some people are like that and they only want a partner as a kind of hanger on, give some thought as to whether you want to be in that kind of relationship),

♥ or they may not be interested at all. You can always ask them if they would like to know something about you, would they like to ask you any questions, would they like to know what you like. You need to make your own decision as to whether you take things further here.

Sometimes just asking people to tell you about their life and what they think is interesting in it is a useful starter. They will then indicate if they feel hard done to and that everyone is against them or if they have overcome problems and are looking for something different.

You can then swap phone numbers and/or ask them if they'd like to meet up again. Your next meeting is usually pretty good either for going for a walk, or meeting in a café, or meeting for lunch. If you have a certain type of restaurant you like to go, it's a good idea to suggest going there, this will give you an indication of how they behave in surroundings you are comfortable in. And if table manners and appropriate behaviours are important to you, you will find out how they behave when they are out and how they eat (do they take their false teeth out, do they talk with their mouth full, or any of those things that you might have to watch everyday of the rest of your life and do you want that?).

Ah and it's important not just from a safety issue (and I hope that you will take all steps to be safe, like meeting in a public place, letting someone know where you will be and what time you will be back), that you think about how much you really want to be there. What do I mean by that? Well just because you want a relationship, it's important that the person you are with "makes you feel good"[3], if you have any feelings of unease or your gut feeling "tells you it's not good" then notice that. Although this book is about you changing your approach, this does not in any way mean that you have to put up with things you don't like or things that don't feel good. It's always good to leave. If something is not right, whether this is the date, or even the relationship. If 6 months down the line something like eating bananas at 2 am every morning, or wearing red PVC underwear, or your partner constantly arriving home late is not what you want. Or your partner constantly putting you down either in public or in private, leave, hey you are entitled to be respected at home. Part of being flexible and understanding the other person is that they need to understand you too.

---

3   On this see page 85 Being Response-able

I mentioned self-esteem earlier – it's about confidence, the circle in a good and resourceful state is one way of creating confidence and you can create it and improve your self-esteem over time. Self-esteem is about being okay with yourself, so liking your body, liking who you are. A relationship is bad when one person tells the other "they can't exist without you" or that they "need you" or you "need them", or if they put you down, abuse you in whatever way, force or persuade you to do things you don't want to do, then leave. No-one deserves to be abused either verbally or physically and being on your own is far better. Just think of how much fun you can have meeting new people, doing new things and if you think all of that is too difficult, my personal suggestion would be find a good therapist/practitioner.[4]

I'll leave the next step in your partner search to you, and remember talking is the best start for any relationship, as they will be many times later you will need to talk, either about where you will live, who will pay the bills, money in general, holidays, friends, nights out, weekend away, children if there are any around or you are going to have some in your lives, relatives, festivities. So start talking from the first second you meet or listening, depending on who starts talking first. And, silence is golden, thinking before you speak, allowing the other person to think before they reply, is also good.

---

4   Have a look at websites such as www.anlp.org, www.professionalguildofnlp, make sure your therapist is qualified, join an NLP Practice Group (you'll meet new friends there too) or take a course, check out www.nlphighland. com for advice too ☺

Getting out there

This section isn't about the transport — it's about setting a goal to get out to meet someone —

What do you want, in respect of this relationship?

Remember to be positive, concentrate on what you want.

Are you willing to start this and are you able to take control of the situation?

Where do you want to have this relationship?

I mean here check out would you be willing to move, town, country (I met a young woman who gave up her relationship [with the father of her child] because she missed her mum and dad and her friends when her partner's job moved him and her to the south of England from Scotland).

Is there anywhere where you wouldn't want to have this relationship? Same applies here; will you be okay living in a Yurt?

What will you see when you have this relationship? (Repeating yourself is good it adds to the practice).

What will you hear when you have this relationship?

What will you feel when you have this relationship?

How will you know when you have this relationship?

Is it appropriate for you to have a relationship right now? Are you in a good place with yourself? If you have children, what are you going to do about them? You do need time for you, but you also need time to get to know the other person and it's best for the children that you sort your relationship out first before introducing your new partner to the children, too many people going in and out of children's lives is sometimes not useful for the children.

So will it look right, sound right and feel right. If it's not the right time at the moment, then can you set a mini outcome so that you will know what to do to as a stepping stone on the way to this relationship?

What do you get out of what you do right now?

Will you need to change what you are doing?

What will you lose? When someone else is around we lose some of things we used to take for granted (someone else in the bathroom, we might have to give some things up). Are you willing and able to compromise? Can you make compromises and negotiate for the other person to compromise and negotiate if necessary? Give and take is good, some of the time.

How will this relationship affect other aspects of your life?

Who and what else will it affect? Will you become so immersed in this relationship that you neglect others, drop your other friendships?

It's a good idea to keep up the things you used to do and to keep your friends and family, because you never know what might happen.

Are there any conditions under which you wouldn't want to go ahead with your partner search or a relationship when you've got it?

You can be better off on your own than in a bad relationship.

What stops you having from having this desired relationship?

Check you have all the skills you need, you've sorted out the past, you've got a good and resourceful state, you've decided on some places to go to get to know people, oh yes and you've started standing up straight and smiling at people. Did I mention that? This standing up to any people. When you look good and get a good response from other people, hey presto, people will like to be around you, unless they prefer to be miserable.

Do you need anything else to start on this search?

What do you need to believe to have this relationship? Do you need to work on changing your beliefs? There's a little more on that later.

What will having this relationship say about you? Will other people notice? Is it important that other people notice?

What will you say about you? Tell yourself that you can do it? You knew all along it was possible.

So when will you start?

And what will your first step be? (As in what will you do first?)

Changing a Belief

I mentioned earlier that our beliefs can shape our lives and we start to filter for and only come across the things we believe, the things we would like are out there, but they are "for other people", "I never get that kind of thing" and sometimes they are smack bang in front of us, or down the road and we miss them. There's the well-recorded story of the natives of an island Columbus discovered who couldn't "see" his ships because they didn't know what ships were and didn't know you could actually sail on the sea, so they couldn't see Columbus and his men arriving and they wondered where these strangers had come from.

So some of our beliefs that have served us well for a long time, are actually holding us back, they are limiting us.

The easiest way to spot limiting beliefs is to listen to the voice in your head when things go badly. Typical examples of the limiting voice in your head are "I'm no good at ...", or "I can't ...". Each time you talk or think in this way, you simply believe it even more.

The good news is that **limiting** beliefs can be changed to beliefs that are truly **empowering** and the following NLP process is a good way to do this:

Write down your limiting belief:

"I never meet the right man/woman."

"No one wants me."

"I can't find the right person."

"I don't know what to do."

Or anything that you keep on saying to yourself.

Look at this statement and ask yourself or better still get a good friend or family member who is a good friend, someone you can trust and either you ask yourself or they ask:-

"What will you get from changing this belief?"

Write the answer down.

Next question "Are you ready to change this limiting belief?

Check that the "yes" is a true yes and feasible. If not, you might need to go back, use the questions we used for setting an outcome (in some cases we are "better doing what we've always done than changing") and sometimes, some people like to wallow in their misery.

Then ask "What would it be most useful to believe, instead?"

Write down the answer.

Now turn it into something you can actually do, so that you are making a start in changing your language so find something you can "do" to make the statement more believable. Use words like begin; start; prepare; establish; grasp; learn; master; realise; understand.

"I can learn how to meet people and be at ease with them". (Because sometimes we need to learn to be at ease with any people)[5]

Make this new "belief" which is going to evolve over time, enjoyable. Find words that would make the belief motivating, such as comfortable; easy; effective; effortless; elegant; enjoyable; fantastic; magical; magnificent; successful; thrilling. E.g. "I can enjoy learning how to meet people and be at ease with them."

Then write down the **final version** of the new belief and notice any objections you might think of (you might not think of any objections, which is ok). If there is anything - then symbolically let it go by writing them down, or saying them out loud, until no more objections are left. They are no longer unconscious.

Now take a minute to imagine living with this new belief for a whole day.

Would it cause any problems?

---

5 [I'm a little worried about 2 children of my acquaintance who are 9 and 12 who can't do anything without mum or dad being there – especially the 12 year old, will mum and dad need to be there on the first date? So learning to be at ease with people is good for you and if you have children it's good for them for you to be at ease with others because children are like little sponges and they copy our behaviours [mm yes granddad in the above case sometimes has to be dragged out of the house] on the other hand we have one 4 year old in the family who is quite happy to stand up in front of a group of complete strangers and talk.

If so, fine-tune the new belief until it causes no problems.

Do a final check: "If I could believe this new belief would I take it?" Check you get a "yes", and that it is truly motivating. Identify what evidence will let you know that this belief is coming true for you. Practise acting "as if" the new belief is yours on a daily basis until it becomes so.

What will be the first evidence that this belief is coming true?

What will you see that shows you this belief is coming true?

What will you hear that tells you this belief is coming true?

And what will you feel that helps you know this belief is coming true?

You may now believe that learning how to change limiting beliefs into empowering ones is an easy, effective and enjoyable skill to master...

Write your new belief down on a piece of paper, a sticky note is even better and keep that in your purse or wallet, on your PC, on the corner of a mirror at home, somewhere where you will see it on a regular basis and be able to read it out loud and repeat it to yourself.

Take all the paper with the writings from the old belief and tear them up and burn them, this way your old belief has gone forever, scattering the ashes makes it even more effective.

Love

"What's love got to do with it", "All you need is love", I want someone to love me, he/she doesn't love me any more, can't find love – all this stuff about love. Love you, love me, don't you love me, she loves me, she loves me not.

You know the thing, or the problem, or the fact is "love" is something you can't put in a wheelbarrow, it means so many things to so many people. Love might be something religious, it might be I love my children, I love my grandchildren, I love chocolate, and a certain brand of ice cream (let's not go there), I love jazz, I used to love my cat (he decided to cross the main road – his name was Merlin he wasn't that magical it transpired), I love my job – but that love thing is different every single time.

What would happen if you start thinking about "love" as a verb, if you're not sure what a verb is - it's a "doing word", so that means how about doing love, so behaving towards other people in a loving manner for example, most importantly what would it be like if you behaved lovingly towards yourself in the first place? We have to love ourselves, if that's difficult then how about some acceptance?

One thing is certain; the only person you can ever change is you. So how about being loving towards yourself, that doesn't mean a whole box of chocolates, or a whole bottle of wine, it does mean looking after yourself and how about putting yourself first? That's not that you are more important than others, but making sure that you look after yourself - and as my Mum once told me "If you're okay then so will everyone else be", well everyone in your immediate environment. Have you noticed when you smile at people, they (mostly) smile back. It works, try it. Have you noticed how when you are nice to people they will be nice to you? Some will be a bit shocked at first - persist. Saying "no" is also useful there, sometimes we say yes to everyone and everything and we lose ourselves in being all things to all people. And that then means that the person you are presenting to everyone else comes across as much happier and other people are happier to be with you, you're easier to be around. (Be aware there will be exceptions to this, as some people are just envious and would like you to be miserable and join them where they are. And there will be people you don't particularly want to be attracted to you, but you can cope with that.)

So how do you attract the right person (for you) into your world and then to you?

What are you good at? What makes you happy? What do you do/have you done that other people tell you makes them happy? Can you do that now?

Make a list, write down what you know you can do well — whether these are household skills, or work skills, caring skills, creative skills, listening skills, can you cut the grass well, make good sandwiches, paint walls, walk dogs, get the neighbour's shopping, pass the time of day with people? Or is it at work where you excel, with colleagues, fixing things for others, leading your team, just doing a good job? So see yourself doing these things and perhaps put them all round you, let each one spiral around you and then place the individual skill, or thing you can do somewhere within a large circle that you imagine to be around you. Notice what it's like when all of these things you see yourself doing spiral, and when they circle, what you see, what you hear, what you feel (if that is appropriate) for each skill you have or thing you do well. Imagine all of these things around you and look at them and notice these are your talents and notice how skilled you are and how well you can do these things and the pleasure you can give other people through doing them. Notice is it important that this person shares everything or some of the things you do or not? And notice what it's like to be you and how competent and confident you are.

It's not what you do;
it's the way that you do it!

Do you know the line from My Fair Lady, "The difference between a lady and a flower girl, is how she's treated."? Eliza, the flower girl, is stating the fact that we treat people differently, in her case because of her appearance and also the way she speaks. Okay, you might be asking, "why is she mentioning that here?" Well it's about how we would like to be treated and also it's about how we treat others.

So remembering I did mention we should think about how we would like our partner to be, the little things that show us, tell us, make us feel "loved" or "wanted", it's a two way thing you know. How will you treat your partner? How will you react when they say or do something, which is "just like everyone else", "just the way your mother/father used to do things" (at some point I have discovered to my own horror, some of us start to sound or even look like our parents), or "all men or all women" do such a thing. Firstly it's not true, not all or everyone does whatever you think they were going to do and it might be true about the parent thing (it's part of the programming by parents, any kind of teacher, significant others, peers at school, college, university or work).

So this new person, or perhaps by now the person in your life, will you treat them differently from others in your life, or will the patterns and habits you've learned in life cause you to respond, the way you always have done, or just the way you did before? I once spoke to a woman who said her partner had told her she was "just like his ex wife", "Really I asked her?" Well no she replied, his ex wife smokes, I don't, she's also an alcoholic, I'm not, I hardly drink, in fact there are lots of other ways in which we are totally unalike. Ah, I wondered, "where do you think the problem lies?" She wasn't quite sure, but she stretched out her relationship with this guy on a line in front of her and actually walked back along this line, she noticed the times when he had "kicked off" (her words) and she noticed actually he had more problems than she did. How did she notice that?

Well I can only suggest that you try it out, imagine a line on the floor in front of you and then think about a point in front of you, which is now. And a point on that line which is, in this case when the relationship started. Then walk from now to that point in time, along the way notice the times when stuff was happening in your life and notice who was there and what you are seeing, hearing and feeling. Note it might be better to step off the line and look at yourself and this experience (these experiences) as a "fly on the wall" — it's sometimes easier to observe yourself than be in the experience. When you've got back to that point either the time when the relationship started, or the time when the problems started, step completely off the line and walk back to now at the side of the line. When you are back at now, step back on the line and look towards the future, your future and check out do you want this stuff to still go on? If yes, it's ok, then just carry on. If no, you have two choices. One you can get out of the relationship or you can take steps to change things.

Now if you want to change things — a few points:

You can't, no matter what you think, or how hard you try, change other people.

You can change the way you react and you can sometimes say some things that will match your partner's way of thinking, so you might be able to get them to see things your way, or get them to sing from the same hymn sheet as you, or perhaps even to understand your feelings! But the most you might get is some temporary understanding and they could then say, ok I understand (and mean it) — but — and you know mostly when you hear that word "but" that they may carry on doing their own thing.

So feel free to change you, and notice is this changing so that you can fit in or adapt to the other person? But you can't change them. So if you want to stay in the relationship it's pretty important that both of you work in it together, couples counselling with just one person does not work. There might be a time or two when one or the other of you needs to work on something private, but mostly it's a good idea to work together.

Anyway back to the start of this section of this book, notice you have a right to be treated in a way that is reasonable, now what's reasonable? Reasonable is in a way that is respectful of both of you, sometimes it's necessary to check out if the way your partner behaves or the things that they say, which you find offensive and hurtful are actually things they "always" do and it's quite commonplace for them. Some things people say in different areas of the UK can be offensive to people from other areas, or simply some things people say and do in some families. Check it out and then firmly and kindly tell them you don't like it. Tone of voice is important, a kind of "pass the salt please" tone is good, make sure you are facing them and remember the matching the body posture. Use a metaphor they will understand. I often explain things to my partner using farming analogies (he's a retired farmer), what will work for your partner?

Remember to treat your partner well, in a way that they would like, as long as it does not compromise you, remember it has to be reasonable for you as well as them; it's about respect for one another. Respect as well when they get on their soapbox, they are entitled to have a rant, and it's important to learn when's a good time to leave the room and how long before you come back and when it's a good time to interrupt or not.

And remember you are entitled to respect as well.

Its okay to say that you find something unreasonable, whether they agree or not. If it's unreasonable for you, you can either negotiate; put it on one side, or worst case scenario, leave. It's handy to check out at the very beginning of a relationship that there won't be things you really don't like, which the other person might think it's okay to do. So make sure you ask them lots of questions, listen to the answers, and spend some time thinking about the answers. Sadly no one can give you a watertight guarantee that the answers you get will be true or the ones you wanted.

Your Ideal Partner

Take a moment to think of who would be your ideal partner.

What would they look like?

What sort of a voice would they have?

How would you feel about them?

How would they act towards you?

How would you act towards them?

Do you have anyone as a model for your ideal partner?

Remember you have to bring something and preferably some things to this relationship, it won't just be up to the other person to sustain the relationship and you can't just put the blame at their door for everything. Or expect that they must do everything to make the relationship work, so why not make a list here of the qualities you have that you will bring to your relationship?

If the word "qualities" gets you stuck, what can you do? Things you know you are good at, or other people tell you they like you for, or things that you think someone else will like. Such as – you can drive, you can plan things well, you like animals, you are good at making salads, you like helping people, you are good at listening, you like computer gaming, anything that you are good at and you enjoy.

I can

1	
2	
3	
4	
5	
6	
7	
8	
9	
10	
11	

12	
13	
14	
15	
16	
17	
18	
19	
20	

Is there anything you would like to improve?

And how can you improve that?

Will you improve this beforehand?

Remember it's not useful to and won't help the relationship if you rely on your partner to help you improve or change your ways. Worst case scenario is you could blame them for your failings; remember you are the only one who can change you.

So think of things you would like to improve about you and make a list:-

I would like to be .... because
....

With this list of things you would like to improve - *Where will you go to get the skills?*

Do you need to make a plan?

Being Okay with Being You

Or having self-esteem, my friend Lucy asked me to write something about self-esteem and about how to be happy with yourself. So I thought I would mention this in this separate section, although I do make references to being okay with being you in various places. Have you noticed them as you've been reading?

So what does it mean, well it's about knowing that you can survive and be happy without a partner, so I don't need a man to be a whole person, I can exist without a man in my life, that is one to live with or be a partner with. In spite of my friend Monica telling me I see you as being in/needing a relationship. Well only if it doesn't drain me/wear me out, do I want to be in a good relationship. And I want that relationship to be good. Good for me and good for my partner.

So if this person you meet says things that you don't like, picks on you because of your size, your accent, the fact you are a little afraid of something, the fact you don't like something, then say I don't like that, that upsets me, I feel unhappy about that, I feel insecure. And if they laugh at you or pick on you even more or just won't let it drop, then it's time to leave, refuse to see them again.

Never allow someone in a relationship, let alone in a relationship you want to have, to persuade you to do something you feel uncomfortable with, unhappy about, you know is wrong (even if they disagree). No-one is worth spending time with if they tell you "you would do that if you liked me", "show me how much you love me and do ....", "you can't possibly like me/love me because ...." anything like that is blackmail and manipulation. People do things for other people because they want to, of their own free will, because they like the other person.

A lot of people end up in bad relationships because they think "they'll never have another chance", "they're too old, fat, thin", "there's no-one of my own sex, faith, race," "I'll go just this once, it'll be okay," "I'll do it, it'll be okay, nothing will happen," or anything of that kind.

So remembering the things you can do, from your list, and remembering that you know to create a good and resourceful state, and be in the present and you can cope with your baggage from the past. Then you can now breathe deeply and stand tall and face the world, being kind, and at the same time firm, and have good self-esteem.

About This Loving Stuff

1	How do you know you are loved by someone else?
2	Can you remember a time when you were totally loved, a specific time?
3	In order to be totally loved, is it necessary for you....
a)	to be taken places and bought things, or to be looked at with that special look?
b)	or that you hear that special tone of voice, or those special words?
c)	or is it necessary that you are touched in a certain way or a certain place?
d)	or that he or she does things for you?

So now that you've thought about that in some detail, notice how sometimes relationships founder because one or the other of you doesn't express his or her "love" in the way the other person in the relationship expects. And sometimes what happens is that we go along for a while because other things are okay in the relationship and then suddenly we explode or act out of character and blame the other person for not showing or expressing their love for us in the way we expect. And the poor other person has no idea what happened because they were just being themselves. My mother used to explode for no reason at all — well none we could understand — something would go wrong — often something minor, so the pans would fall out of the cupboard and one of us would be stood nearby and suddenly for no accountable reason - because we hadn't moved, after all we hadn't touched the pans and we could very well be in the wrong for touching them now, — mum would exclaim "well you could help, you can see I'm having a problem" — mmm.

I like to be taken places and bought things, like little things like cards and insignificant gifts (well to some people that would be the case). I realised a short while into my present relationship that my partner doesn't do the cards and gifts, he likes to get them, but he doesn't do the giving of them (to me) he does do things like giving me lift up the road (and I need the exercise), like not letting me drive his car (because he wants to treat me like a lady and spoil me in that way), that he enjoys doing the shopping (wow, yes please), hanging the washing out (he's a dream — well there are things he does that I don't like). So I changed my beliefs on "how someone shows me that he loves me" and I spend more time noticing that we do things I like — such as eating out by the sea on a warm and sunny evening, and going up to the top of a hill to watch the sun set and dawn break at midsummer. Who needs a fluffy toy? You can't change someone else, but you can change the way you react. Knights in armour on shining white horses, or pretty damsels, who want to do your every bidding, are in short supply, especially in the 21st Century! And "a dream" or "a dream man or woman" will always be just that – a dream. We can allow our dreams to become reality, by noticing that the guy or gal in front of you has wonderful qualities. Have you seen the film Shrek?

And there are other people around who send me cards and thank yous, my grandsons, clients, and I can make collages myself, and buy me little things I like. So the better I understand myself and what I think I would like, the better I am able to understand my partner and I can therefore create a more satisfying and pleasurable relationship.

Now sometimes I may have to repeat myself, several times. Just how many times? You know we have patterns, run patterns in the way we are convinced of things. Sometimes we say that this is nagging, we have to nag someone – but do we?

What happens if we match the other person's body posture and use a tone of voice that is "normal"- so we leave out the whining, complaining, commanding, demanding, whatever it is that "turns the other person off" and we state our case, taking into account some of the following?

So does your partner need to "see something, hear something, do something or read something" in order for it to "sink in". I have a couple of friends when I want to get my point across to them, I need to write to them, one knows it works for him and he told me so several years ago and asked me to write to him so he could understand something better, and the other one, asked me "why do you write to me, when you're really annoyed? You know I have to take you seriously." Well what do you say to that?

And, or – does your partner need a number of examples, so

do you need to present (so say it, write it down, show them or show by doing) them with the information, or will they react when presented with partial information, or are they never completely convinced, they need to re-assess the information each time (yes there are people like that, and it's not their fault, it's just the way they are), or does the information need to remain constant for some period of time? Now it may be that they react differently for different pieces of information, in different situations, or maybe that they react in the same way for everything. You only need to work it out if you are having problems, honestly. Only if something isn't working, do something else instead.

It's really worth giving all of this thought, especially when all the other bits of your relationship add up (see my list near the beginning of this) so why throw it all away because you don't bring me flowers as the song says ?

Okay ....

you might now be saying, or perhaps screaming and how am I supposed to find someone?

Would you like to change your wish for a new partner into a want and from that want get what you really, really want and what you truly deserve?

First up 2 things — if you are British, or English or Scottish or Welsh or you have just been brought up in a way that means you are polite — you just might believe (ah yes beliefs again) that asking for what you want is wrong. "Want doesn't get" or something like that. Well if we wish — we could become a bit wishy-washy and we'll keep on chugging along and things will keep on not happening. Believe me it is okay to want, as long as it's "ecological" — that means it doesn't affect those around you (your family and friends, neighbours etc.) in a detrimental way. And the bottom line is unless we start to want things we just won't get them. No one who has made anything out of their lives spends much time "wishing".

Okay off soapbox.

Starting on the way to Getting What You Want

I'd like to ask you to think of something in your life that is undeniably true, that you have, that you know is yours and that you are quite clear about.

Got it?

Step 1

So when you have it, what does it look like?

Where do you see it?

Near or far?

Clear or fuzzy?

Colour or black and white?

Picture or panoramic?

What do you see there?

Is there anyone else there?

Is there anything else?

Do you hear anything?

Is anyone saying anything?

Are you saying anything?

Are they any other sounds?

Are they near or far?

Soft or loud?

Rhythmical or monotone?

Is there anything else?

Are there any feelings?

Are they in your body or external?

Still or moving?

Do they have a shape or size?

Do they have a temperature?

It's really useful to make a note of your answers to all of these on a sheet of paper and even better to get a really good friend to help you do this.

Put all of those answers on one side and have cup of tea or something like that.

Step 2

Think of something, which at the moment you wish for, so we're assuming this is a relationship — and ask those questions of this thing you wish for, I've repeated the questions here below — write the answers on a separate sheet of paper.

This relationship you wish for -

What does it look like?

Where do you see it?

Near or far?

Clear or fuzzy?

Colour or black and white?

Picture or panoramic?

What do you see there?

Is there anyone else there?

Is there anything else?

Do you hear anything?

Is anyone saying anything?

Are you saying anything?

Are they any other sounds?

Are they near or far?

Soft or loud?

Rhythmical or monotone?

Is there anything else?

Are there any feelings?

Are they in your body or external?

Still or moving?

Do they have a shape or size?

Do they have a temperature?

Step 3

Now at this point get the list you wrote down when you very first started reading this book (see page 9) - the list of 20 things you wrote earlier in this book, it might be useful as well.

Take the 2 lists, so the list of answers in respect of this thing that is undeniably true, that you have, that you know is yours and that you are quite clear about. What is there on that list that is so very different from what you wish for, what is exciting about that thing that is undeniably true?

Taking these things that are very different, that are positive, so they may be for example — close, clear, in colour, positive things that you or others are saying, what was your reaction to things if they were soft or loud or rhythmical or monotone? — whichever one was positive is the right one for you. Now put some of these positive things into your re-presentation of this relationship you wish for.

Example — my thing I know undeniably to be true is based around my work, so lots of people, lots of bright colours, lots of movement, music, warmth, a really warm feeling because I'm getting good feedback, and I feel whole.

So we (my friend Linda helped here again) worked with me on my wish for a relationship — for me in this it was far away and fuzzy (I couldn't "see" this man yet) and there was no sound and it was cold.

So Linda invited me to put colour in this relationship and bring it closer and to perhaps add some of the things from my list of things I wanted in the relationship (it's always handy to check out some of these things that we think we want, as sometimes we like the idea of something and then when we get it we didn't really want it), she invited me to make it clearer and add other people to it, she invited me to add music to it and warmth.

And I did. And you know what? I started to want this relationship. And the following night we went out and Linda "fixed it for me". Hey even at my age 54 then, and even being someone who can talk to anyone, anywhere at any time, speaking to a fella whom I might like to start a relationship with, was - daunting. But more about that later.

I hasten to add, I didn't just go out for any man. There had been 4 in the frame at one point, one I knew very little about, but he was a bit shy, and one actually found someone else, and one I hadn't seen for a while and I was pretty sure that this one (my partner now) fitted a lot of my criteria, I had a friend who said so. And we had talked on several occasions, we sometimes had a communication problem, but that's because he speaks Doric some of the time, and sometimes he just doesn't listen and I think that's an art at times!

Always, Everyone, Every Time
(How to keep the relationship)

Whilst I was writing this, I had a learning moment or a few days actually, I decided I wanted to leave my relationship. _____ Keep on reading.

I had a crisis, well I thought I did. Part of it was down to the fact that I deleted some bits of information, and I distorted some others, and I generalised a bit and best of all (some sarcasm required here!) I repeated some or at least one pattern, or we might call that a habit.

The main details are not important here, what is important - goes in this order.

The next day I emailed a friend, a good friend, whom we had been out with 2 nights before, and I said to her – "I don't think I'm qualified to write this book anymore, because I think I made a mistake and I want out of my relationship." Linda, I've mentioned her before, wrote back, "well perhaps that's something you need to include in the book anyway. It's not just about how to find the relationship, it's also important to keep it. So perhaps you could work on that."

Mmm, interesting I thought. And I thought some more, and I went over what had happened the previous day. And I realised I was worried about something over which I had no control. You know those things, you can think of one or two. And then I realised there were a few things that I had got angry about (you know those kind of things – the kind of things the ones that "make you" react in a certain way, the things that people say that "make you" do things). Well did you also know that only you have control over you, only you can allow your buttons to be pushed; only you are driving your bus? The bottom line is you have the choice to decide how to react. Now so often in the past we have reacted in a way that has not been useful. We like life to be easy, so we react that way again and again and as in the case of the beliefs – it just happens and we get the same reaction from us and others as we have always had. So when your partner behaves "just like your ex", or "just like everyone else", or you "just knew this would happen", or "all men or all women are the same". Well basically it's because what we expect to happen will happen, so when we "play safe" and "expect the worst" – then guess what? That's just what we get. (Remember Beliefs!)

Think about it – if you smile others will smile, "laugh and the world laughs with you, cry and you cry alone". If you snap at people, they will not like you.

So back to me. I realised, when I thought about it, that my relationship was at "that stage, for me, where I hit a bump". So then what happens is, that something happens in my life and I go into the depths of despair and look for everything that is negative and bad (in my own world) and I delete all the good things, I distort a few things out of all proportion and I generalise a thing or two. Have you seen the film "The Holiday" - beautiful young woman wants to run out of a relationship - know that one? I thought that was a great film in respect of relationships and so are "Bridget Jones' Diary", "Sleepless in Seattle" to name another two, you can think of more.

And I forget all the things that attracted me to my partner, and I forget the warmth and strength, oh yes and that he's attracted to me, and I forget I have good friends and I forget I do good things with other people and I forget to have patience.

I also occasionally forget to use the stuff I'm good at, which includes listening and understanding and questioning what others mean when they talk to me. So in our relationship we both have our own understanding of what we mean by "relationship". I would like to get married (living happily ever after is not a given), and my partner's idea of relationship is that we are good company, and fortunately that also means that grumpiness is allowed and it's mainly me that's grumpy (he's a man of the world). He only really gets annoyed about being overcharged and bad driving (that's another story — did you know we all have blind spots?).

So what I'm saying is it's important we learn to understand the bits of conversation we all (and that's a generalisation too) delete. Some questions for improving understanding:

"What is the most useful question I can ask, right now?"
"What don't I know yet that could make the most difference?"

"What is the most useful way to think about this?"

"What wants to happen here, and which question is the key?"

"What question can I ask that will be most useful to the other person?"

Ask yourself these questions or one of these questions in your head. Spaces in conversations are fine and whilst you're thinking - put aside any assumptions you might have about the other person's face pulling, grimacing etc., and those thoughts you "just know what they are thinking" (there will be times when "knowing what the other person is thinking is useful" – however when you have a heated discussion this kind of knowing or assuming is not useful, believe me).

Like some suggestions?

"What is the most useful question I can ask, right now?"

Sometimes it's about stopping thinking about me and instead thinking about the other person, you know they might have had a hard day at work, they might be feeling really bad because someone has scraped their car, or they might be tired. So ask questions like "how are you?", "how was your day?", "what can I do for you" – and then like the answer even if it is I'd like to be alone for a while (leaving someone alone saves arguments), or if they ask you to do something you don't want to do at that point in time, negotiate it for later, would it be okay to do that later?

"What don't I know yet that could make the most difference?"

Well the answer to this could be one of the above questions. But it just might be for example if you have reacted badly to some other person in your partner's life, that this other person is important (even if you don't like them, can't stand them — interfering is not good you could lose your relationship — the better part of valour is to say okay, and in a quiet voice I don't like them, and let them go to wherever it is). [I do the Mickey Mouse thing here — see next chapter]. So it might be find out how much this person, this thing in the house, this ritual means to your partner and work out how you are going to cope with it.

"What is the most useful way to think about this?"

I suppose I could use the last piece as an example - I put it on one side is one thing. I also remember that I can use it as an example if my partner objects to something I do (said of course in the "pass the salt tone") "remember you do your paper delivery". (He delivers a paper to a long-standing friend — don't ask me why, but notice it's a long-standing friend and that's important to him). What does it mean to the other person? Are you big enough to accept it is good for them and it's not detracting from who you are, or what you do, and most importantly from your relationship.

"What wants to happen here, and which question is the key?"

Well what might it be useful to do, walk out the room? Calm down, come back, say you are sorry.

"What question can I ask that will be most useful to the other person?"

One of the best things I have ever said in my personal life - when I was really at my wits end and unable to put my best professional thinking head on, or be a "fly on the wall" and look at what was happening between us from a different perspective (with a lot of practice it can be done in a heated discussion) — I said "I really need you to help me, I need you to talk here — because I just don't know what to do." And the answer I got was so far re- moved from anything I could have expected, or "known", or assumed, because it had absolutely nothing to do with me, and it explained my partner's problems and gave us a basis to move forwards and things became even better for both of is, because we knew we could talk even more and do something. Instead of getting stuck in his reasoning, which we had been and that was according to him - we had a problem, because he had been on his own for a long time and was stuck in his ways.

Facts were, he wasn't stuck, and he was using that as an excuse to stay in a comfort zone that is a pattern for not having to deal with something. And the other very real fact that came straight into my head when he said that was — excuse me I've "been on my own a lot longer than you".

Now often we forget the facts, and in relationships we allow the fog — stuff that someone says (someone, could be ourselves, partner, the media, TV soap characters, our family, convention …..need I go on?), past experiences (remember the baggage and what to do with that?), laziness and complacency and more to get in the way.

As I was talking about this book and the ideas behind it to someone else, we'll call her Jane (that isn't her name) — I noticed she was making some comments and whilst I watched her thinking (I know her pretty well and how she processes thoughts and experiences) — I asked myself — mm what nerve am I touching here? So I asked her "Jane, you know I wonder just how many people who have been in relationships for a long time — meaning 20, 25 years or more (nowadays I sometimes think 10 years is a long time for many people, but that's another subject and maybe this book will help some people to revisit their relationship and think again and strengthen the relationship with their once loved one?), well I wonder how many people grow apart because they hide behind the fog?"

"Fog" — now there's a word — what do I mean by that? Well I've used that as a generalisation for times or words or actions that we hide behind. In any relationship we grow, and we change, over time we can then become complacent and often we are complacent in the way that we lull ourselves into thinking we are right, the other person is wrong, we have done everything we needed to, we should do and we don't actually sit down and talk, or ask questions, or think we might be the one who is doing something wrong. We have our own interests and sometimes we think they should come first and really it's just a way of hiding from confrontation.

Talking is good, arguing can sometimes be good, and making up is a really good idea. So finding a good and resourceful state and saying calmly what you want out of life, and from your partner is a really good idea and perhaps if they're not willing to listen, or talk and compromise then perhaps they're not the right person?

The problem with words is they do not have a fixed meaning; they have the meaning we attribute to them. Ask 3 or 4 or more people in the same room to describe each of these things separately - Elephant, Alarm, Velvet, Lemon and Smoke – I guarantee you that you will come up with different interpretations and even if some of them sound the same, then ask a few more questions about their description; as people's understanding will give different pictures, sounds and feelings. Simply ask them to describe in more detail. What implications does this have for everyday conversation?

Tonight my partner on the phone to one of his daughter's asked me "do you like pork" – I answered "we had pork for lunch" – which meant in my head "yes dear, of course I like pork, don't you remember?" – he relayed "we had pork for lunch" – daughter said "we can have something else" – err no, that wasn't what I meant – argh!

When we use language, we set frames of reference - these frames establish our reality or models of the world. Language is a symbolic system and for that reason never becomes reality. To deal with the world we map by choosing the information that suits us and we use the map to move through life - in doing this we use Distortions, Deletions and Generalisations. We need to do this, we couldn't survive otherwise — information overload.

So we delete — we choose to remember bits of what we experience and leave parts out. We either don't register them or write them off as unimportant. Have you ever looked for your keys then found them in a place in which you already looked? That's how deletion works.

So in a bad mood, or on a day when something has thrown us, we only hear the negative in what others say and delete the positive, even when they are both in the same sentence.

We distort — we change our experience, exaggerate it or reduce it and see it in different ways, like a hall of mirrors in a fairground does.

If we weren't able to distort we wouldn't be able to be creative. It is useful to be able to imagine what something will look like when it is finished, redecorating a room, decorating a cake for example. Those are positive aspects of distortion. If you make the decision that the way someone says, or writes something, or looks at you, means that they don't like you, you run the risk of creating a distortion of reality and distorting your response. "I know you don't like me, you're looking at me the way my mother does when she's angry (and it might be the sun's in their eyes). Fantasy builds on fantasy.

We generalise, we take aspects of an experience we have had as representing a whole class of experiences and ignore any exceptions. This can be useful to help us respond to new situations on the basis of similar ones in the past. It causes problems if we generalise wrongly or do not stay open to a new experience. Beliefs are examples of generalisations. I used to believe all men were useless. My son told me, I hadn't met ones who were useful yet, and of course I was concentrating on the wrong thing.

When we generalise we do it in order to make sense of the world and to help us to know what to expect. This means we know that things shaped like chairs will be something to sit on and give us support. It is part of how we learn. But the same process can be disastrous, if we have had a difficult relationship and decide on that basis that all men and women are the same – untrustworthy for example, then this generalisation could stop you from forming any relationship with anyone who is an exception to your rule that you have created.

People who distort their experience can be a constant surprise with their interpretations of your actions and words. They make unusual connections and tend to "read your mind" or "know what you are thinking" and assume they know your thoughts and feelings from what you say. Artists and writers often use distortion to create fantasy worlds; of course we can use distortion to get things so wrong in life!
People who generalise a great deal can either be very sure or very unsure or insecure. The world can seem very simple to them - black and white, shades of grey are not so easy for them to work with, an experience for them has to be one thing or the other

A thing with Mickey Mouse

Is there someone in your life who is annoying? Start with someone mildly irritating. Imagine an image of them out in front of you and push that image further away, if you need to actually do the pushing physically, then do it. Drain any colour out make the image sepia or black and white, push the image further away, several miles in your imagination, it's your imagination you can do what you like. As the image of this person you used to dislike gets further away, add a pair of Mickey Mouse ears to this image and a big red nose and give it a squeaky Donald Duck voice. What's that like now?

You more your practise this, you just might find they are easier to cope with. Very useful for irritating people from your past

Criteria

These are the things that are important to us, our values. There's a useful, and I think important piece of information here – you can actually be friends with people who have different values to you and you don't have to share their values or subscribe to them, but you can agree to differ and still take the good qualities from that friendship or relationship. Other useful things about Criteria or Values are, we can have different ones at work to at home and that's okay too, but we do need to have congruent ones, so you do need to be able to say to your children or your partner or other significant others I value honesty and be honest with them, as honest as you want them to be with you for example. However we can't demand that others have our values and criteria just because we'd like them to – I might like the world to share my values but I can only put my values into practice and hope that some people will follow.

So if we look at my list from the beginning - what are my values in there?

Single – yes that's a value
Money – yes that's a value – if you don't value money it won't be in your life

Hygiene — do I need to say anything?
Likes music — this can be a value
Is fun to be with and has a sense of humour — fun is a definite value
Likes closeness and hugs — is a value
Is open — Openness is a value
Is truthful — Honesty is a value
Non-smoker — what do I value here? health?
Likes sex (with me — only) - loyalty

Now my work values are different, with some similarity

The order varies at times

Money
Making a Difference
Customer Satisfaction
Honesty
Loyalty
Teamwork
Support

I could for example have a relationship where money is unimportant, but for work it's different. I once used to work for nothing or very little, that has various drawbacks. But what is important for me is that I have a plan for which I want to use the money I will earn and other people will benefit from this, my family will be a minority in this, and they will also benefit, but the far reaching consequences are greater for others. So money is an important value at work in respect of what it will provide for others and also in terms of payment from companies where my skills and those of my colleagues are of great use.

Being Response-able

A useful tip as well in respect of reactions to "things" that happen. No one can "make" you do anything, so comments like "every time you do that you make me", "that just made me", "people like that make me" – all of those statements are really just an excuse – we are refusing to be response-able. It's useful to remember that you are in control and therefore when someone else does something you have a choice to respond or not and when you respond it can also be useful to remember that you are response-able. Able to respond in a way that is appropriate for you. So when someone you are getting to know says or does something and it starts to "make you" react in some way, perhaps you can use the "bubble" (as in "Being in the Present") use the "circle" (as in "A Good and Resourceful State"), think about what to ask next or question what the other person is saying (in your head first and think about the tonality, the words, your body posture). Check out is this some "programmed" reaction from the past? How important is this person to you? Would you be willing to change your response, are you willing and able to make this change to the way you respond? And become able to respond in a better way.

Please and Sorry (how to have a way with words)

You know please is an interesting word, in some languages it's not needed, because it's understood by the way you ask something that you are being polite. So you might ask would you do something for me, or would you like to do something, or may I have something, and in those even in the English language "please" is really implied. It's just an extra word, which (in many languages) we don't need to use, as we have the right tone and body posture, so that the person we are asking to do something knows we are being polite. In the English language we get hung up (sometimes) on the use of the word please. Other times we forget to use it at all, and there we have problems too.

Now why am I waffling about this? Well if the prospective partner in your relationship does not speak British English, then notice they may not use the word "please" as often as you might like, or you might have been trained, or programmed to believe is necessary by your parents, teachers, peers etc. to believe "please"[6] should be acceptable. Notice

---

6   Whilst we're here those phrases "you know what you should do" or suchlike "should" denotes often someone else's idea of how they or someone else thinks behaviour is supposed to be, and often if you question this, the answer you get is, "well everybody does it that way". It might be useful to question what they are actually saying, either out loud or to yourself and decide how to respond.

how they look at you, what their body posture is like, what their voice tonality is like, do you need the word "please", in order to continue?

Conversely overuse of the word "please" or phrases such as "pretty please" can make things sound a little over the top. Sometimes simply altering your tonality, looking at the person whilst you are speaking to them (eye contact is not always necessary – some people think better when they don't look you directly in the face). Looking at people is often useful; especially if they have hearing problems and many people do find hearing clearly in situations where there is background noise, conversation or music difficult. Looking at them makes it easier for them to locate the fact that a) you are speaking and b) that you are speaking to them. And then asking the person "if they would" do something for us, or "might do", is actually more effective and less obsequious, as long as you are congruent and definite (not aggressive).

Now "sorry". Sorry is one of the easiest words to say in any language, what is difficult to do for a great many people, is actually to mean that they are sorry and to either act on what they have said or even to carry it out.

What does this mean for a relationship? Well it's really constructive for a relationship to be very careful with your use of the word. I had a lodger once (I've had several lodgers over the years –it's often good to have someone to take care of the house or help out in other ways) – this lodger was a young woman who had experienced some interesting things in her life. Anyway she believed "sorry" was an answer for everything, "sorry I'm going on holiday and I can't pay you the rent for 2 weeks, cos I need it for spending money", "sorry my boyfriend climbed up the drainpipe last night and it broke off", and many, many other sorrys. The thing was many things then happened again and again.

Do you or does someone you know use "sorry" as a throwaway word and then just either carry on doing whatever it is "squeezing the toothpaste tube in the wrong way", "eating your chocolate", "reading your paper first/or folding it the wrong the way", or worse,[7] and then they keep on doing it again? Well we can't change the way other people act, but we can change ourselves, so if you say "sorry" frequently, how about changing that into "oops" or whatever you might choose to say and explain what you've done wrong, actually putting your hands up to having done something wrong is a big thing, and believe me it's actually much easier, as you don't have to live with the guilt or the thoughts of "I wish I hadn't done that" and you can also do something about making up for what you did, or doing something differently!

Thank you, remember to say thank you and sometimes it's useful to show your gratitude, but if someone doesn't "pay you back" – "buy you a coffee" because you bought them one – it doesn't mean that they are ungrateful, it might mean they simply said "thank you" and they meant it. Also please bear in mind, most people do things for you just because they want to – it doesn't mean you have to "spend the same amount of money", "cook the same meal", "buy them the same kind of present" – if you want to do something for them – remember you talents. What could you do for that other person? Wash their windows, dig their garden, take their dog for a walk, take some photos, give them a lift somewhere, wash their dishes for a week (yes please). And you can always write them out a "promise to ....", tie that up in a red ribbon and give it to them.

---

7   We may have had the experience of people who hit us and say "sorry", I
    won't do it again. And guess what?

Why did you do that?

Why? That's a very useful question word when you are small with which you can learn to negotiate the world and find out "why things work or happen in a certain way". In later life it can become a problem. When someone asks you "why" - do you sometimes feel yourself "going on the back foot", "becoming defensive?" That's quite a normal response. And then what happens? ....

Notice what happens when you ask "How did that happen?" I can give you 2 examples here. A friend of mine, who is a hotel manager, mentioned in conversation about a hotel he had recently taken over that at lunchtime in the bistro there was a problem. Every time sandwiches were ordered with a hot meal, then sandwiches would come out curling at the edges. He had asked the chef "why" this was happening and each time the chef became defensive. I suggested he ask the chef "how" does this happen. A month or so later I saw my friend again and, as so often happens, when I asked him if he'd tried my suggestion out, he said, "gosh I forgot to tell you", I asked the chef "how" and his reaction was completely different, he relaxed, looked surprised and explained to me how he would do things differently next time.

The other example comes from my daughter, and really refers to "who did that? Which is another question that sends us straight into an "I'm in trouble mode." At a friend's house with her children, my 3 year old grandson and the friend's 2 year old daughter were playing upstairs in the bedroom. There was a loud crash, the 2 friends dashed up stairs and discovered 2 guilty looking toddlers in the room, along with a smashed plastic crate. Friend asked "Who did that?", the children blamed one another. My daughter asked "How did it happen?" My grandson took hold of another crate, turned it upside down and began to show how both of them had stood on the crate and jumped up and down and it had broken.

Might changing some of what you have been saying and some of how you have been thinking and/or talking to yourself make life a little easier for you? As well as making starting up and retaining relationships with others?

So where you feel tempted to ask, "Why did you do that?" even asking yourself that question (not just other people) — we do that when we want to find an excuse for what we do, use "how did you do that" and the answer to that gives you a process, and you might come up with a way of doing things differently for yourself or you might just understand other people and how they work better. And how will that affect your relationships?

Sometimes just putting something on one side and getting on with life is far more useful than "why". At the time of writing this, I just met up with a friend who about 16 months ago took exception to something I said[8], and her response was

---

8   There's another NLP Operating Belief here "The meaning of your communication is the response you get" - *This may be different from the one you intended.*

indeed different to the one I had intended (see "Mails and Other Forms of Communication Killers" for some more information on this). And she "threw her toys out of the pram" and wouldn't speak to me, I left a few messages with other people, as she wouldn't answer my phone calls (caller display can work against the person calling), and I waited. Fortunately the friendship was an important one and still is (sometimes friendships aren't important enough or the other person or you are "not in the right place", "life gets in the way whilst you're planning other things" [in the immortal words of John Lennon]). And eventually 16 months later she spotted my daughter in a nightclub and walked up to Kris and spoke to her and eventually asked "How's your Mum?", to cut a long story short, Kris said "she's fine, she would love to hear from you." Also Kris told me this, now I know Mary (that's not her name) well enough to know that she would spend several more days, weeks, even months getting round to contacting me and a little voice in her head would be giving her 30 thousand reasons why she might not do it at this moment in time, so I sent her a text, we both had time when we could put other things on one side, me writing this book and she tidying the house as her sons were away and we met up and caught up, it took about 5 hours and we still haven't finished. We've both moved house, I have many new things in my life. And hopefully she will have many new things in her life, thanks to her move. And our friendship is moving forwards. We did briefly mention the point at which she stopped speaking and neither of us could really understand it, so we moved on in our conversation and in our friendship.

A good friend is someone you can think aloud in front of, a good friend is there to pick up the pieces and a good friend will always welcome you back, a really good friend will also put their foot down and say I don't like that (whatever it is you might be saying or doing - like your latest fad or partner) but you know it's okay I still value you as a friend. My oldest friendship goes back to age 11 when I started Grammar school, she phones me when she needs to talk and I know if I need her she will be there for me, she also came to my second wedding (see the end of this book if you need to) and she came to Michael's funeral, she just said "I'd like to be there". My other very good friend I've known since I was 16, we were pen friends at school, she's in a different country, if I need her she is there, when I go to visit them I usually get taken along to "sort something out", I also get taken to school (she's a head teacher) — we listen to one another's worries, and we go to the Opera, I don't that in the UK, well rarely.

Friends are important, it's important they are non-judgemental (after all we are only judging from what we believe to be true, it might or might not be true for us, but it certainly ain't true for the other person). Friendship is kind of like the most precious balloon you ever had as a child, let it fly and bounce on the wind at the end of a string and if you pull it close, treat it with care, because if you squeeze too hard it will burst into pieces and you can't, however hard you try put a balloon together again. You will need your friends on the way to your relationship, you will need them in your relationship, and you will need them after your relationship, nothing is so good it lasts eternally — do you know these lyrics?:

"Nothing is so good it lasts eternally
Perfect situations must go wrong
No-one in your life is with you constantly
No-one is completely on your side"

They are from "I know him so well" from the musical Chess and there are more lyrics than this and I've taken these out of context, but for a reason. At some point your partner or you may leave the relationship. If we marry, we marry "till death do us part" and that I think is possibly the "nicest" (said with great care here) way for a relationship to end. For some people relationships will end earlier than we would like them to. This can be due to death which happens at an untimely stage (I don't really think there's right time to die – it hurts the people who are left at any age). For some people it will be someone else's death that ends the relationship, the death of a child, another loved one, sometimes one partner becomes so ill they are no longer the person you met and partners make (for me) interesting choices about how to deal with this situation. Some people are just not the right people at the time, and we have to acknowledge that and move on.

With a lot of work, and it takes a lot of work to sustain any relationship, you will keep the relationship and that includes your friends. This year a young woman on one of my courses whose marriage was a few months away set her "Life Purpose" and in that she stated something along the lines that her husband to be would have to be there for her to fulfill her life purpose. The guy on the course working with her came to me and asked "is that okay, I thought it's a good idea to have in this only things we can have on control over (or we reasonably believe we can) and not to rely on other people". Yes he was right, so I took Sarah (that's not her name) on one side, as she was already starting to get upset at the thought that her future husband might die. Now I am in the position (if you haven't been to the end of the book you might want to peek now or just believe me) to say, hey people die. The love of your life can die (or just walk out) and you might be stood there saying (shaking like a jelly and falling apart) I can't go on, and if your life purpose is that you can't continue to live without that special person, you will be stuck, very stuck.

So a) nurture your friends, notice they are not more important than but just as important as your relationship and b) make sure your partner is a friend!

Mails and Other Forms of Communication Killers

Mails or emails and text messages can be a nightmare or a minefield, whatever metaphor you choose to use here.

Emails are missing out emphasis, irony, humour, anything that is included in telephone and face to face conversations, they are also often written in abbreviated form and can be sent off in the heat of the moment and even worse……….. they are tantamount to worldwide publishing within seconds, one click of the mouse and your comments can be sent worldwide and if you continuously forward previous emails on, someone, somewhere might read something you didn't want them to read.

And text messages well can u txt? And cn u read txts? And I don't even know if I've missed out the right bits.

With texts and emails it's also possible to send them to the wrong person, by clicking the wrong button!!!!!

How to be friends

It's important to be friends with this person you meet, now whether you both decide to jump into bed with one another on the first night, or not until later whenever that may be, is entirely up to both of you (I stress both) it really must be mutual consent and because you want to have sex with this person. I'm not here to suggest when is a good or bad time to have your first sexual encounter with one another. (And please when you do have your first sexual encounter my friend Linda would ask me to remind you whatever age you are, to make sure sex is safe, wear a condom [and there are condoms for females too — Linda showed me them — it's part of the job she does]).

But it's really important to be friends, friends have respect for one another, friends don't mind when you say "do you mind leaving the room whilst me and my mate talk personal things?", friends are willing to talk about anything that you want to talk about, they keep their opinion out, they don't say "you know what you should do", "what you ought to do is", they will give you're their opinion if asked and whether they'll expect you to follow it or not, is up to them. Also as a friend it's only useful some of the time to say "I know exactly what you mean" [you probably don't know "exactly" what they mean and it could lead to problems]. Assuming you know what someone else means can be fatal, you then go and do one thing and they are doing something else. As a friend, don't expect people to follow your advice, they might only have been using you as a sounding board. Friends will smile and say "you're on your soapbox again" and possibly beat a hasty retreat but they won't fall out with you because of your opinion. They will warn other people not to "get you started" about something and more fool other people if they do get you started, because the friend has already warned you.

It's important to like or love someone because of who they are (as a person) and not because of what they do or what material wealth they have or how they look, and it's important to have respect for them. There are certain things my partner does which I really don't like and I notice my reaction to them and sometimes I sound off about these things, sometimes he doesn't hear me, sometimes he ignores me, sometimes I catch myself starting to say something or react in a certain way and I stop myself if I can. Life is really too short to argue about the way he does something just because I have "always" done it in a different way.

I realise my life and the way I was brought up and grew up are very different to that of other people and I believe my "filters" are perhaps quite broad, of course someone will tell me that it is untrue and I have been told I'm intolerant (what me?). There are certain things I refuse to tolerate and I will tell people politely and firmly. For some people I have noticed whether they are in a call centre or in a shop (and this is from watching other people) — if you speak firmly and state your case in a no nonsense way this is classed as "abusive" or "getting upset". Interesting.

There's a "frame" I often use "interesting what does that mean for the other person?" and sometimes asking myself that question stops me and gives me time to think. Or "what on earth did they do that for?", I don't need to know the answer but I have stopped and thought and time has passed and I go onto the next "pass the salt" – sounding bit of my conversation or simply breathe and carry on.

Friends are so important, I'm not sure if the reason so many people drink too much, get stressed etc. is nowadays that we don't really do talking, share things with friends, not just what happened in the latest soap or what's happening with the neighbours etc. but just talking for the sake of talking. That when something goes wrong or we need something we don't have a circle of friends (a network) with whom we can chat, and discuss, and who will help us – this all links in with "Where can I meet someone" and the piece about thank yous. Real friends expect nothing in return and they give friendship unconditionally. Real friends will get up in the night and when they realise it's you they will say "hi – how can I help you?". Real friends will drop things and help you and that's the kind of friendships it would be really good to strive for in your relationships. Real friendships are where each one does what they are good at and sometimes the other person helps if you can't do something, for whatever reason. What's wrong with beans on toast for the whole family if your wife is not well on New Year's Day?

If you "can't communicate" ask yourself why. Is it you, or is it your partner, or is it both of you? As I've already said the only person you have control over is you, so what can you do to change things?

A Map to Navigate By

I've mentioned operating beliefs, I think they are quite good to navigate by – Johnny Depp's character Captain Jack Sparrow has a compass, this compass shows you where you want to go, similar to Lyra's compass in The Northern Lights (the film The Golden Compass) which only Lyra can interpret as she has the skills. This book can give you the skills to go where you want to go to, by believing you can do it, by believing in yourself, you've set up your list of what you want in a partner, you've decided what you can do well, you've thought about where you might go to, you know that other people act differently and you are equipped to work with that and yourself so perhaps these maxims might be useful.

People respond to their map of reality and not to reality itself.

I mentioned maps or models of the world before. Remember how you experience something will not be the same as your partner, there's no need for you to experience things the way they do. But you do need to appreciate that they are different and that's okay.

There is a reason for everything people do.

We're not always conscious of what the purpose is, so sometimes acknowledging I was an idiot at that point in time (or he/she was) and moving on is really helpful.

All behaviour has a positive intention.

Yes honestly, it really does, we're always trying to achieve something valuable for us. But a person is not their behaviour, and that's important to acknowledge early on, if you think you are a lousy speller, reader, homemaker, lover, person full stop. It's probably because some (un)kind person said that you were lousy or bad at something at some point and you keep on reinforcing the behaviour. We tell children to behave — excuse me, how would you like them to behave — they are behaving even when they are behaving badly. So the child "behaves" then gets into trouble for that behaviour and is told you are a bad child, a naughty child, or worse and the message then becomes embedded in the mind and people mess up. So my behaviour is not always me.

Having choice is better than not having choice.

If you continuously look around for choices for yourself to make you more flexible you will have the greatest flexibility of thought and behaviour, and then you will be able to influence what is happening in any relationship you choose to have. Narrow thinking prevents us from meeting new people.

People make the best choice they can at the time.

You know when you do something and you wonder why on earth you did that or you wish you hadn't done that (little speech bubbles might appear out of your head when you replay the scene later — if you replay in cartoon form). This also applies to other people, so no matter how self-defeating, bizarre or evil the behaviour, it was the best choice available to that person at that time that fitted in with their map of the world. Offer them a better choice in a way that is appropriate for them and they will take it, it could be make or break in your relationship.

People work perfectly.

No one is wrong or broken, yes really, after all they've practised doing what they do for years (Jim has a very irritating habit — to me, and I've come to the conclusion he's done it for years and I'm fighting a losing battle trying to get him to stop — life's too short). What is important is to find out how the person functions, and then you might be able to change it into something more useful and desirable, for that person — it is important that it's for them not for you. Remember the only person you can change is you.

The meaning of your communication is the response you get.

This may be different from the one you intended. There are no failures in communication, only responses and feedback. So the response you get is feedback, it might be they are in a bad place or it might be you are, what are you going to do about it? Every response and experience from that response can be used. If you are not getting the result you want, do something different.

We already have all the resources we need or we can create them.

We looked at what do you want, knowing what you want is a resource, we worked on what things can you do, what are you good at, this is a resource, friends are resources, and good and useful states are resources too.

Modelling successful performance leads to excellence.

You can take skills you have in one area and apply them to another, so you might be good with people at work, but think you can't meet a partner, err how do you go about meeting new people at work? I had a problem with this; I can talk to anyone, but chat Jim up the first time, apart from a little intro from my friend (Linda) I also needed to remember a good and resourceful state from when I meet new people in a business context. Guess what? It worked.

We process all information through our senses.

Some people will see what you mean, will paint you a picture, others will be on your wavelength, what you say will strike a chord with them and others will get a good feeling about you and feel things are going the right way. Notice that, notice when times are challenging is my partner processing differently to me, do I need to show him how to do something rather than talk him through or do I need to walk him/her through it step by step?

If you want to understand – act.

Get on with it, try it if it doesn't work first time you have feedback to do it differently next time☺.

Making it last

Everything I've said in this book will enable your relationship to last. It's perhaps useful to ensure that you have give and take in relationships but equally, it's most useful to talk and ask questions. If you think you are being overlooked, ignored, hard done to, something is not fair, then ask. Sit him or her down or go out to neutral territory, where it is quiet, where you can talk, notice if you "always" have arguments in the same place, after the same thing happens that he or she does, at the same time (of the month — take hormones into account, also when the money is running low). Remember Jane — who feels she and her husband have grown apart and also there's Wendy (not her name) who says "she is not in a nice relationship" — over the past few years he goes to the pub and gets drunk, he doesn't actually talk to many people, let alone her, he comes home and he grumbles and she grumbles too, but they don't talk to one another.

After a while, a while in this case is when you or the other person start to notice that things are "the same", are "getting stale" — make a date to go out, to do something different, so different might be a different restaurant, different pub, might mean a walk instead of a drive, might mean going to a football match because one of you likes football or rugby or darts or dominoes, or a different kind of film or the theatre instead of a film.

I like jazz; we sometimes go to Country and Western. Last year we went away for the weekend, my daughter knew we had been shopping and about the food we had eaten. Later that month Kristin was on a course with me where it was mentioned what NLP calls our Map or Model of the World (that's how we remain sane by knowing what we know and understanding things from our perspective, everyone has one, and they are all different). On the course I mentioned how we sort or filter for what's important for us and I said Jim and I had been away, in Jim's version the most important event of the weekend was we went to a football match. A voice came out of the participants (totally unrehearsed) "You went to a football match, you didn't tell me". I hadn't told Kris because it wasn't as important (to me) as the clothes and the food. For Jim's last birthday we went to another football match, it was a surprise in as much as I didn't ask him what he wanted I looked to see when there was a match that I could go to with him (he didn't have to take me) and double whammy was that it was one where two teams he likes (he's a generous guy) were playing one another and with a little help from a friend (I had to ask a policeman) I got the tickets. I enjoyed the match – I made sure there was nothing else happening that day, it was his day and off we went well wrapped up for the occasion.

The pay off is that Jim will do things that I like, and I'm proud to have him with me. Ah yes, I'm proud to have him with me, not because "I need him" or because "I have to have a partner to be a whole person", but because I like him, he's warm hearted and generous (with many things), he's more forgiving than I am, for me he's a very calm and grounding person and he can talk to anyone (he sometimes has to get over that hurdle, I know some interesting people in some interesting places, and am quite happy to speak to anyone — mostly to prove I can and most people like to be spoken to), he's there when I need hugs and I've become a much calmer, and a little more forgiving person[9]

So what's stopping you?

---

9   Someone told me recently I set high standards for myself and therefore everyone else, not really - there's another NLP Operating Belief/Presupposition "if one person can do something, anyone can" — which means you don't have to do it the way I do and you don't have to get to my standard, but the one that is right for you in this relationship.

A Tibetan Meditation

1. Take into account that great love and great achievements involve great risk.
2. When you lose, don't lose the lesson
3. Follow the three Rs: Respect of self, Respect of others; Responsibility for your actions.
4. Remember that not getting what you want is sometimes a wonderful stroke of luck.
5. Learn the rules so that you know how to break them properly.
6. Don't let a little dispute ruin a great friendship.
7. When you realise you've made a mistake, take immediate steps to put it right.
8. Spend some time alone every day.
9. Open your arms to change, but don't let go of your values.
10. Remember silence is sometimes the best answer.
11. Live a good, honourable life. When the time comes reflect on this, you'll enjoy it a second time.
12. A loving atmosphere in your home is the foundation for your life.
13. In disagreements with loved ones, deal only with the current situation. Don't bring up the past.
14. Share your knowledge. It's a way to achieve immortality.

15. Be gentle with the earth, and respectful of the seas and rivers.

16. Once a year, go somewhere you've never been before.

17. The best relationship is one in which your love for each other exceeds your need for each other.

18. Judge your success by what you give up in order to get it.

19. Approach love and cooking with reckless abandon

20. Love as if you've never been hurt.

Original Source Unknown

So, what happened to me?

Why am I qualified to write all of this?

Well I left home at 18 and a bit years old, and went to live in Germany. Why did I leave? Well I was bit sick of my Dad's attitude towards me and some other stuff that happened in my life, like not being listened to. Things have changed; considerably, I would like to add at this point in time.

Well after some time, I met a German guy and I married him about 3 weeks before my 20th birthday. About 3 to 4 weeks later he began to stop out all night and sometimes all day, drinking and to be abusive (verbally) and crash around, he was also handy at accusing me of having problems and hang ups!

November a year later, he went off to London for the day (he had won a competition) and I stayed at home because it was a local holiday. I didn't feel too good and didn't do much in the flat and when my then husband got back from his day trip, he went a little over the top and threw me against the edge of the door frame damaging my back, and I had to go to the hospital.

Well life went on for a while, quite a while, and he disappeared now and again and told me various stories about what he was doing which seemed to be plausible. I believed at that time that I had married for life and that I had to make a go of it and that I needed to be in this relationship to be someone. So on my own I was insignificant.

At the last company I worked for in Germany I was one of only 3 women amongst about 40 men and I was on good terms with all of them because I was in charge of checking their expenses, amongst other things. Over time I became attracted to a guy at work and things could have gone further but they didn't. He was 10 years older than me, very sensible and talked to me about the time I was left on my own and made me aware that I had problems with my self esteem but I didn't know what that was then and I didn't believe him anyway.

My daughter was born in 1976 (my husband disappeared for the day, the day after she was born!) and then I was ill after she was born and we returned to the UK, the best things about my first marriage (yes first — there was more than one — keep reading) are my 2 children.

In 1979 I discovered that money had gone missing from our joint savings account and when I questioned my husband about it, it resulted in a row, in which I was thumped in the ribs and they were fractured — I did badly bruise his thumb! He took me to hospital and afterwards showered love and affection on me and my daughter, and he bought us presents, and he told me he loved me and would never hurt me again. And I believed him. And he didn't, well not physically.

We moved house, and this was after someone I worked with

in a local restaurant told me my husband had "tried it on with her" at the Christmas party, I said "Oh he's a friendly guy".

My son was born in 1980 and then a string of accusations of "indecent assault" against my husband happened and in October 1982, the 16th actually, I left the marriage with my two children.

And if I knew then, or even before then what I know now.

— according to my brother, - I have two failed marriages, now the first one, for me was a huge learning curve and one to get out of and I'm very grateful for my children — but the second marriage, well Michael died and I don't think either of us can be blamed for a failure there.

Right at the start of our relationship Michael and I had a conversation about death. Death hey I'm only 38, you're 40 why are we talking about death? Had I known then what I know now, I might have talked some more. But the conversation we had went on Michael's side along these lines, "Rosie, if I ever become so ill that I end up in a wheelchair, or can't take care of myself, I don't want you to look after me, I want you to have a life of your own and go out and be a success and enjoy life."

We had only known one another a few weeks. I said yes, okay and actually didn't question it.

It was a dizzy spin, this relationship, he was a wonderful person, he liked everybody, sometimes too much as he would give people anything and he had time for people. He had time for my children too and only entered into the relationship after he had made sure they liked him too — note to you if you prospective partner has children at home, get them on your side. If they are old enough to have their own lives it has nothing to do with them what your partner does (unless you are mistreating or defrauding them!).

He moved us in with him very quickly (with hindsight he perhaps knew he wasn't going to around for long). He was just there. There to argue with, there to make love to, there to go on holiday with, there to entertain friends with, there to visit people with, there to go on business trips with, there to help me alongside me when I was teaching German.

Oh yes I had followed Clare Rayner's advice and I had gone to do something I enjoyed, I joined the local German Circle, a group of people who met each Sunday evening and talked about German and Germany, their common theme was they liked Germany and/or spoke, or were German speakers. The first night I managed to make it, was a "Party Night" and "Mike" wasn't there. I found the others intriguing and the subject was one I love anyway.

The next time I went, some nutter in jeans and denim jacket and "white" trainer boots was there, he had a shock of black hair, he seemed to be quite loud and this trainer boots seemed to wave about a lot. The next time I was there and so was he (and unknown to me he had asked the chairman to introduce us). It turned out Mike had lived in Germany and spoke passable German and we chatted. The next time it was the German circle, he came and sat next to me, I moved, he moved, I couldn't get rid of him. The older members chuckled in amusement. I offered to take him "out on the car park" to sort him out (men seem to think this is funny — hey guys I mean I will sort you out). He then asked me out for a drink afterwards. And later we went to his house which he showed me proudly and I lent me the "catalogue" to his music cassette collection. Now this catalogue was of course unique, not something he could replace and he insisted I take it home, because of course he would have a reason to get in touch with me and ask for the catalogue back. And he took me home to my house and made sure I went in the door of the house. So he knew where I lived and he had a reason for us to get in touch again ☺

Well, after almost 2 happy years, he started to act strangely and I was on the point of leaving him, because in spite of me repeatedly saying, there is something wrong, and he did go the GP and the GP asked him if he always been like this and Michael said yes, he didn't know that there was anything wrong.

One day he came home from work with a headache, the headache got worse, to cut a long story short, Michael died a year and 5 days later, as the result of a brain tumour that had sat itself on the top of the brain stem and the back of the optic nerve, operating on which would have killed him or paralysed him at least down one side. (And he had said - "Rosie, if I ever become so ill that I end up in a wheelchair, or can't take care of myself, I don't want you to look after me, I want you to have a life of your own and go out and be a success and enjoy life.")

Well the last 3 things took a while and I have
a life of my own
I am a success
and I do really enjoy life

And I have a wonderful partner

You can have that too ☺

(Or the same/ similar as my grandson Leon Michael age almost 4 would say)

Glossary of NLP Terms

Anchor – link of a stimulus with a response, a user friendly form of Pavlovian condition, connecting an automatic unconditioned response with a condition one.

Associated – mentally seeing, hearing, and feeling from inside an experience, in contrast to dissociated (seeing a representation from the outside, as a spectator).

Congruence – When goals, thoughts and behaviours are all in agreement.

Beliefs –generalisations about yourself and/or the world

Break State –Doing something different – i.e. say your telephone number backwards, "what did you have for breakfast?" – ensures that you can move onto something else or a different part of a technique/process.

Criteria – Standards you use to evaluate something – what's important to you?

Dissociated – stepping apart from, and out of, an experience, seeing or hearing something from a spectator's point of view.

Ecology – The question about the overall relationship between idea, skill, responses and larger environment or system. Internal ecology, the overall relationship between person and thoughts, strategies, behaviours, capabilities, values and beliefs. The dynamic balance of elements in a system. Checking to see if something fits, is useful, productive, enhancing.

Frame(s) – Frames of reference, the ideas, experience, people we use as a reference to create meaning as we travel through life.

Neuro Linguistic Programming (NLP) – The process of creating human excellence in which the usefulness, not the truthfulness, is the most important criterion for success. The study of the structure of subjective experience. It is a process developed by a group of individuals who wished to explore new perceptions of reality and gain practical methods for themselves and others to develop their thinking, well-being and success. NLP now embraces many ideas and "tools" taken and adapted from many other disciplines. These tools are useful in self-development.

NLP Presuppositions – (Operating Beliefs) – Principles or assumptions on which NLP is based.

Resourceful State – The total neurological and physical experience when a person feels resourceful, confident, and able to cope effectively.

Sensory Modalities – the five senses through which we experience the world, sight, hearing, touch, taste and smell.

Timeline – The unconscious arrangement of a person's past memories and future expectations. Typically seen as a "line" of images.

Values – see criteria

Bibliography

James & Woodsmall, Timeline Therapy and the Basis of
Personality
Meta Publications 1988

L Michael Hall, Meta States
Neuro Semantics 1995

Prior and O'Connor,   NLP & Relationships
element 2000

O'Connor and Seymour, Introducing NLP
element 1993

Shelle Rose Charvet, Words that Change Minds
Kendal Hunt 1995